We're going to have your tongue tie released. This will help you eat and breathe easier. Let's talk about what happens when you get a tongue tie release.

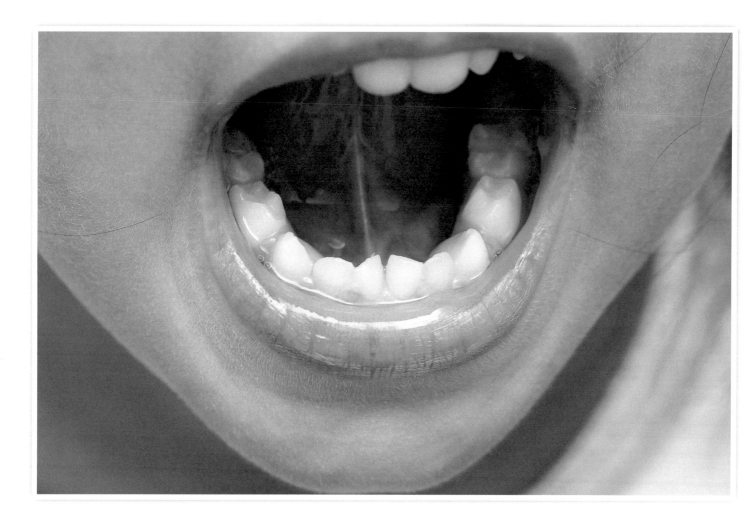

Your tongue has a little band underneath to keep it in place. Sometimes, it's too tight and makes it hard for you to move your tongue.

A tongue tie release is when a doctor fixes the band so you can breathe better and eat all the yummy foods that help you grow.

When it's time to go, you can bring your favorite stuffed animal or blanket to snuggle.

At the doctor's office, we check in at the front desk.

There may be important papers for me to fill out. You can play with toys or read a book while you wait patiently.

When it's your turn, the assistant will call your name and take you to the back. Don't worry - I will be waiting for you when you're all done!

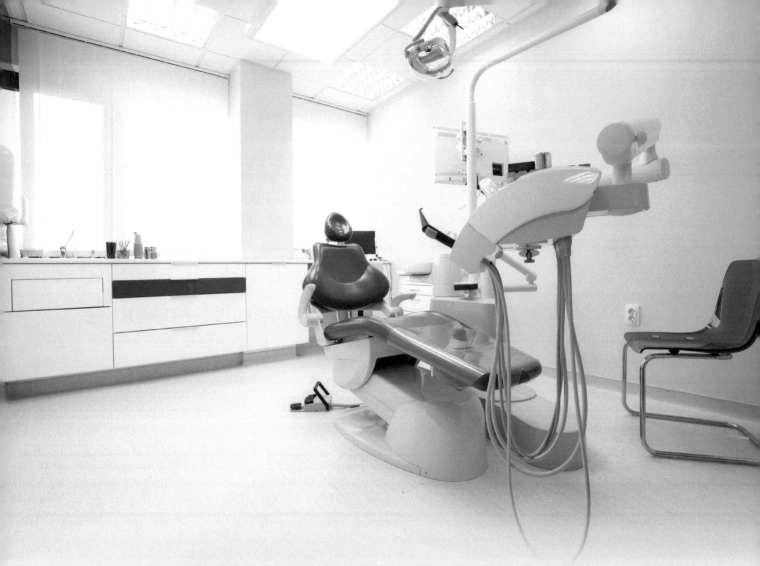

Next, you go into the exam room. Inside there is a special chair for you to sit in and lots of instruments for the doctor to use.

The chair is really fun. It moves up and down and you get to lay all the way back.

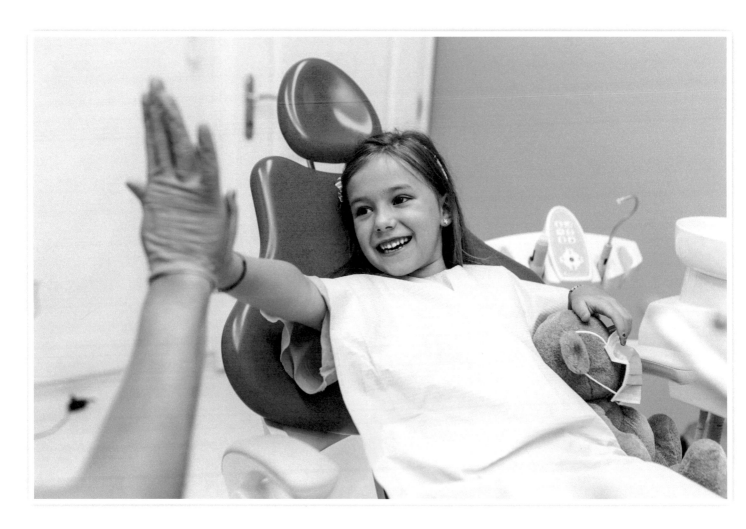

Once you're comfy in the chair, the assistant will put a bib on you to keep your clothes clean.

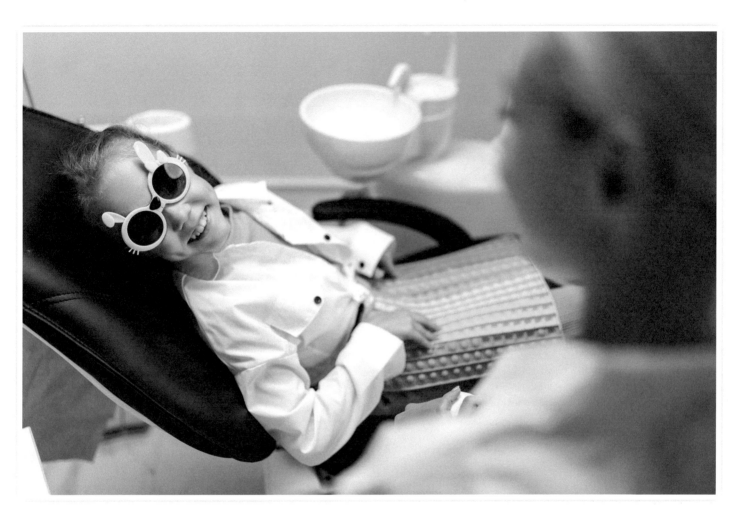

You will also wear sunglasses to protect your eyes from the light and use a bite pillow to help keep your mouth open.

Then, the doctor uses a cotton swab to put a numbing cream on your tongue. It may tingle a little bit or make it feel like your tongue is asleep!

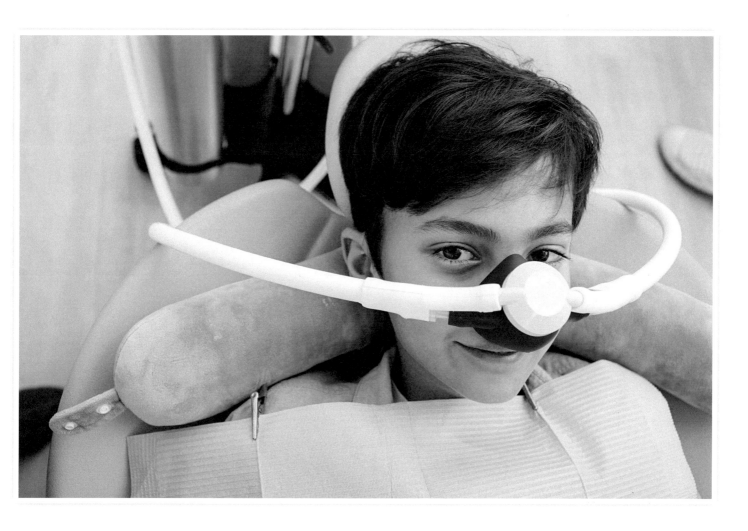

Sometimes, you take extra medicine or wear a funny mask on your face that will help your body feel calm and relaxed.

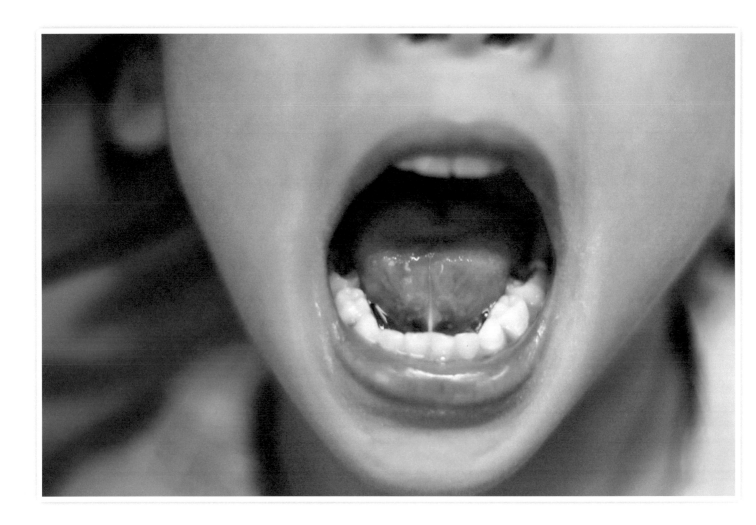

Next, the doctor will use their instruments to release your tongue tie. It's important to hold very still.

When it's all done, the doctor's assistant will bring you back out to the waiting room where I'm ready to give you a hug.

You may feel a little grumpy or your tongue may feel different. That's okay — you can rest or cuddle with me.

If you're hungry, you will get to eat some of your favorite soft, tasty foods.

We also get to do tongue stretches to help your tongue get stronger.

Now you're ready to go get a tongue tie release!

About Dr. Kacie M. Culotta

Dr. Kacie M. Culotta

DR. KACIE M. CULOTTA
DENTIST - ORAL TIE RELEASES

Dr. Culotta believes a healthy child grows into a healthy adult. Her comprehensive and collaborative philosophy ensures your child is set on a path to long-term wellness, beginning with a healthy airway, free of oral dysfunction. When she's not with her patients, she treasures her time with her spouse and their two wonderful young daughters.

Dr. Culotta is located in Austin, Texas.
Visit LatchedBeginnings.com to learn more about Dr. Culotta and her practice.
Follow her on Instagram on @Latched_Beginnings

Made in the USA
Columbia, SC
08 October 2024